Come As You Are

Also by Mark Snyder:

Epitaph: A Conceptual Elegy

Necessary Evil

(experimental music)

Requiem

(a secular conceptualist setting of the Mass)

now available on iTunes, Amazon, and elsewhere

Come as you are, as you were, as I want you to be...

as a friend, as an old memory...

And I swear that I don't have a gun.

-Kurt Cobain, "Come As You Are," 1991

Come As You Are

Mark Snyder

RADICAL TOTALITY

2014

Copyright © 2014 by Mark Snyder.

All rights reserved. This book or any portion thereof may not be reproduced or used in any manner whatsoever without the express written permission of the publisher except for the use of brief quotations in a book review or scholarly journal.

First Printing: 2014

ISBN-13:   978-0692227039 (Radical Totality)

ISBN-10:   0692227032

Radical Totality
764 Seven Lakes North
West End, NC 27376

radicaltotality@gmail.com

For Mike Benedict-

I miss you. I'm not gonna crack.

I sing
unrelenting hate
exiled,

doubtful

sure
fathers

hate;
For what offense
persecute

spite

but far away,

long causes
lay behind;
Deep in her heart

distant
remnants of
long years unhappy

scarce
left behind
with

fury

revengeful

whirlwinds from beneath

awful
majesty
ruined

fury
restless
living

captive
pressing for release,

rage

driving
fear of
their fury to those dark abodes,

wandering slaves,

my enemies.

duty binds me to

your pleasure,

with confusion
And
fearful cries

trembling

the sound
Of raging   breaking
          fearing
          awful
          majesty;

                    insolence

you shall be taught obedience

To rest
       the living
    descend

              repeated

dying
   into life,   they rise,

              lie along the ground:
       infected

Our hope

promised

your doom reversed,

secure renewed

serene

kiss

of Fate

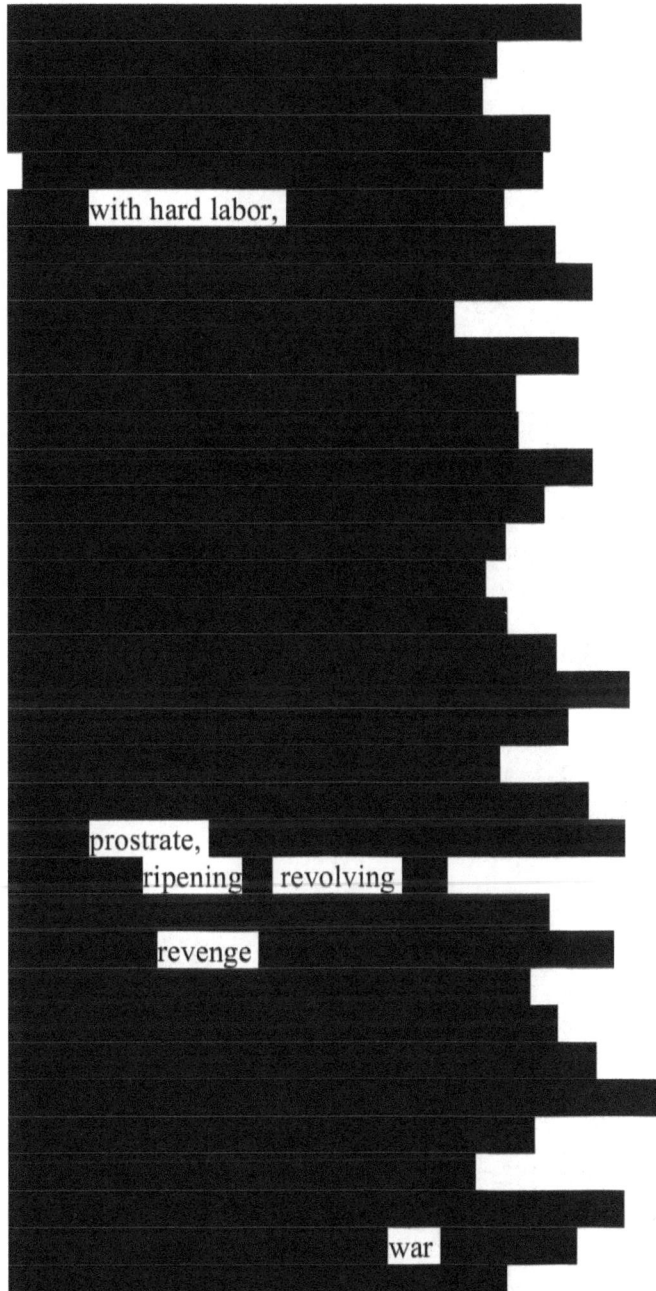

with hard labor,

prostrate,
   ripening   revolving

revenge

war

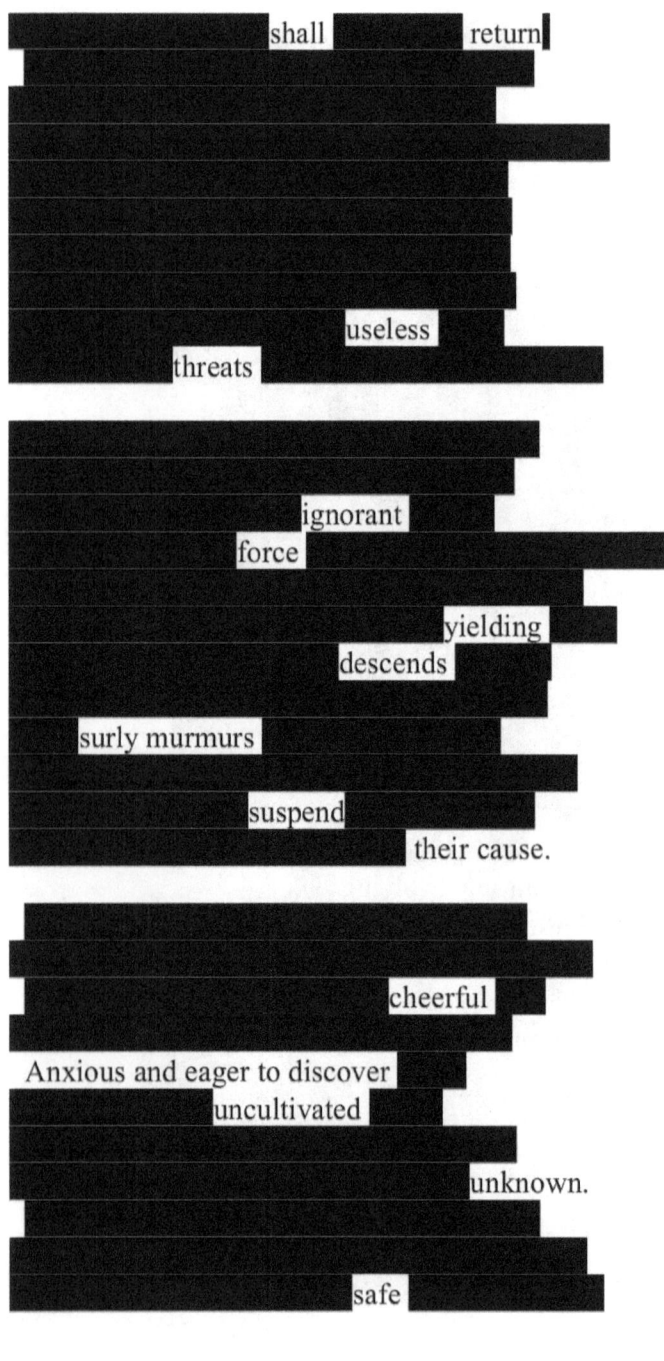

shall return

useless
threats

ignorant
force
yielding
descends
surly murmurs
suspend
their cause.

cheerful
Anxious and eager to discover
uncultivated
unknown.
safe

recesses

wanton
quiver

mortal

stranger,
who commands
wretched
victims

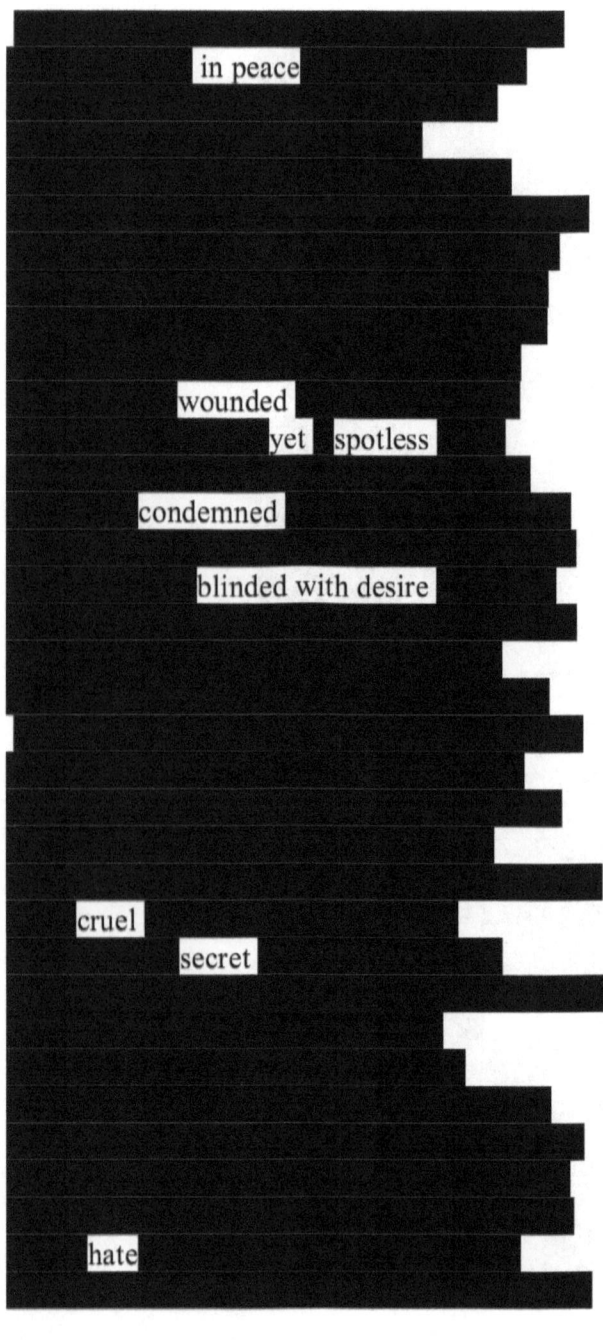

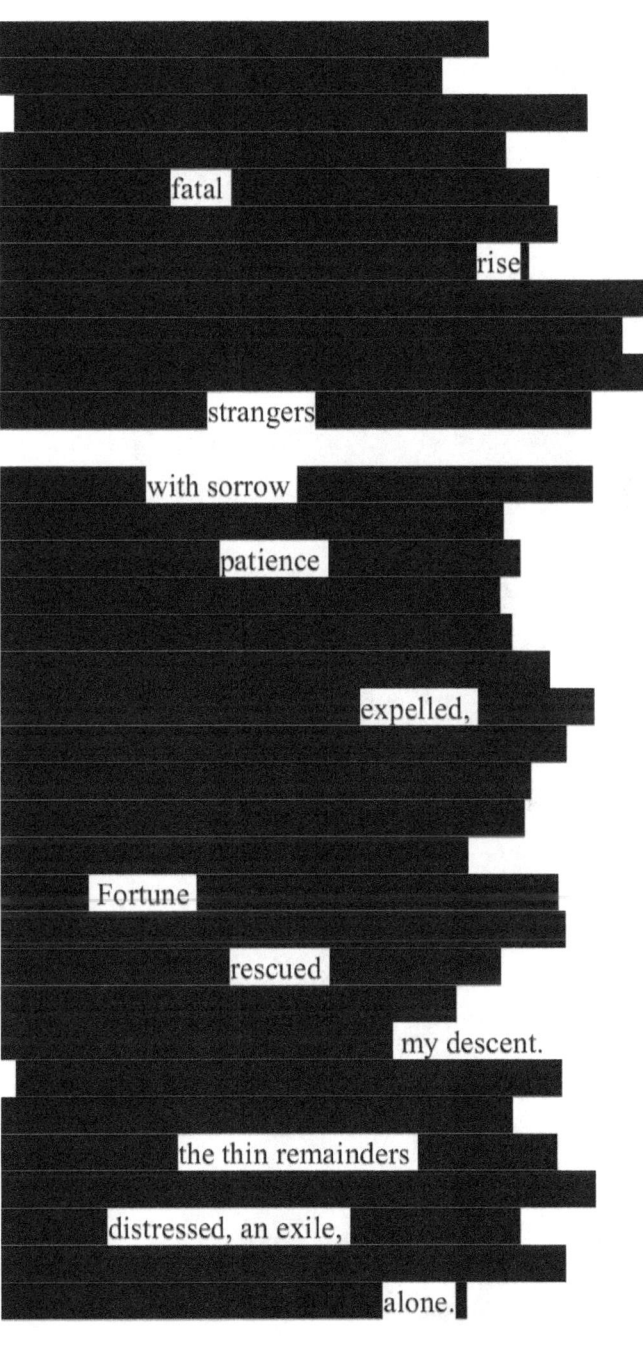

fatal

rise

strangers

with sorrow

patience

expelled,

Fortune

rescued

my descent.

the thin remainders

distressed, an exile,

alone.

friendly
courage

renounce

the clouds

with joy

otherwise

pursue

The path before you

cruel

embrace

lazy

Concealed
unmarked
unseen

Thick
holy
omen

fated

solemn
consecrate,

expelled.

fierce
    weeping
monuments

Devouring
    an empty
        fainting
        trembling
            driving
                grief
            whose cruel

            boy
Hung
        sticking in his wound,
With tracks of blood

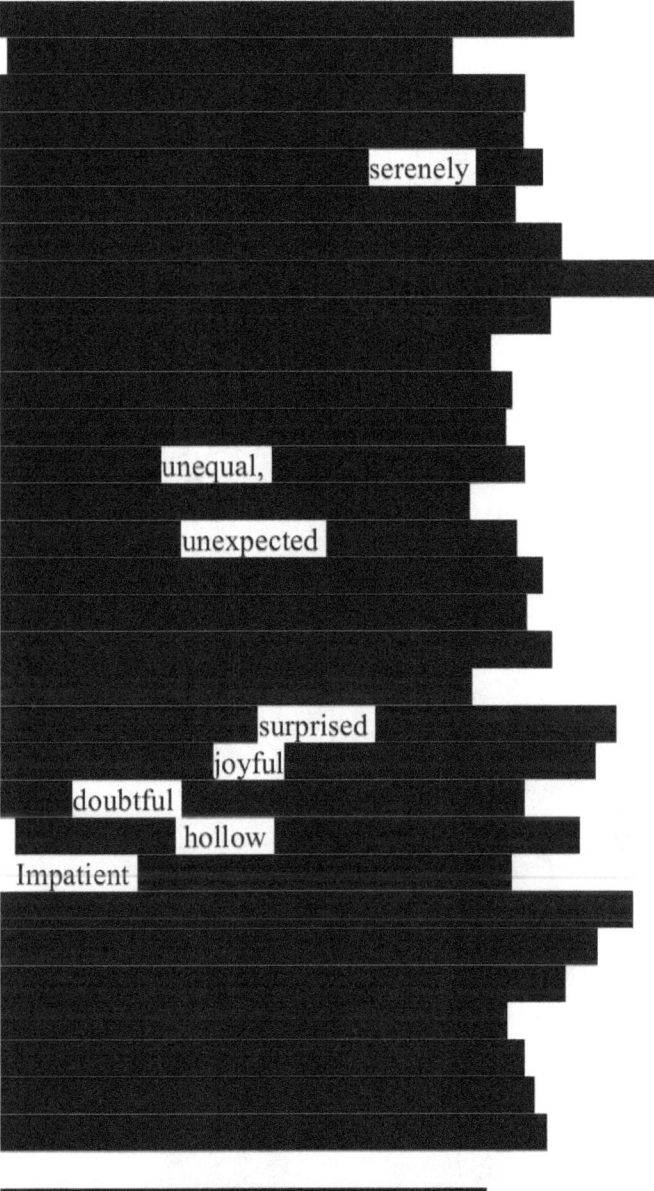

serenely

unequal,
unexpected

surprised
joyful
doubtful
hollow
Impatient

wretched clemency
the remnant of wasteful

winds

drowning
compassion
and revenge

renew

friendly

cries

dismiss your fears;   cruel fate

You seek

to defend

the Storm,

your wandering

dissolved

sparkling

radiant

life

scattered

acts of mercy

gave you birth.

Your honor shall never die.

what angry

lineage
bore
into my mind,
my father's

siege

And his own ancestry

For I like you, have been distressed,
an alien in a land unknown,

curious

precious gifts, the boy

came

To ruin

revengeful
force

A love so violent,
neither can change,

love's disastrous insatiate, tumultuous joy,

The dead

rage

silence

to ratify the peace.

eclipses

I will restrain my tears

with delight

destiny required
the monster
to
explore
The vulgar

madness

hollow
blind secret

Trust

trembling

fated

captive

To impose on their belief, obstinately
To die

Trembling
his haggard eyes
receive
a wretched fugitive
Scorned abandoned

our passions die.

fear
ordains my words

to lie.

Accused and sentenced for pretended crimes,

the wretched

boy,

In private mourned
Mad
With silent grief,

my guilt

just revenge

My death will   please,
And set   at ease
                     broken

hearts
trembling   renewed,
With   fear,

this dreadful answer

sought,
your safe return

sacrifice
dumb
clamors

I
Was destined by the wrathful god to die.

I broke my bonds and fled the fatal blow.

what further hopes for me remain,

now free,

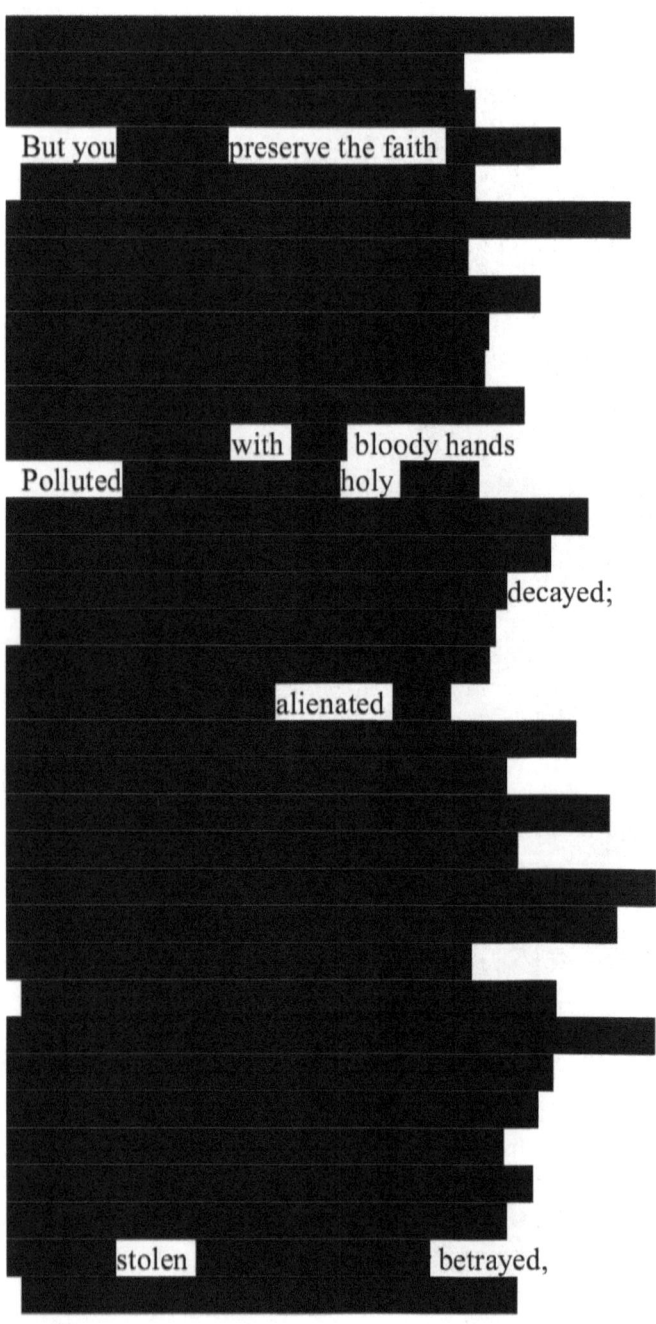

forbidden

hopes   lost;

so religion and   god ordain,
if you violate with hands profane
        you   shall burn,

sharpened fangs   limbs and bodies grind.
wretched
his gasping throat
holy   venom
breaks   yielding
doomed to die
dared to violate the sacred
destruction.

by god's decree,
none believed

the silent night,

joyful

nameless   forces
        oppressed

Those few

the dead

A bloody shroud

visionary

champion,

wearied

After so many funerals

What new disgrace

groaning

mournful words

The flames and horrors of this fatal night.

The noise

Louder,

the frightful sounds

deluges

destroy   pain

wasteful ravage

The sound
　　frenzy
　　　　　　resolved to die
But first to gather friends,

　　　　wrathful　　　irrevocable doom

finds him

Come, finish what our cruel fates ordain.

And heaven's protecting powers are deaf to prayers.

Resolved, in death, the last extremes

Night was our friend; our leader was despair.

Houses and holy temples float in blood,

take new courage from despair and night:

unknowing

mistaken disdain,

With fury

awful impious
testimony

I strove to have deserved the death I sought.

Renewed in courage

weary

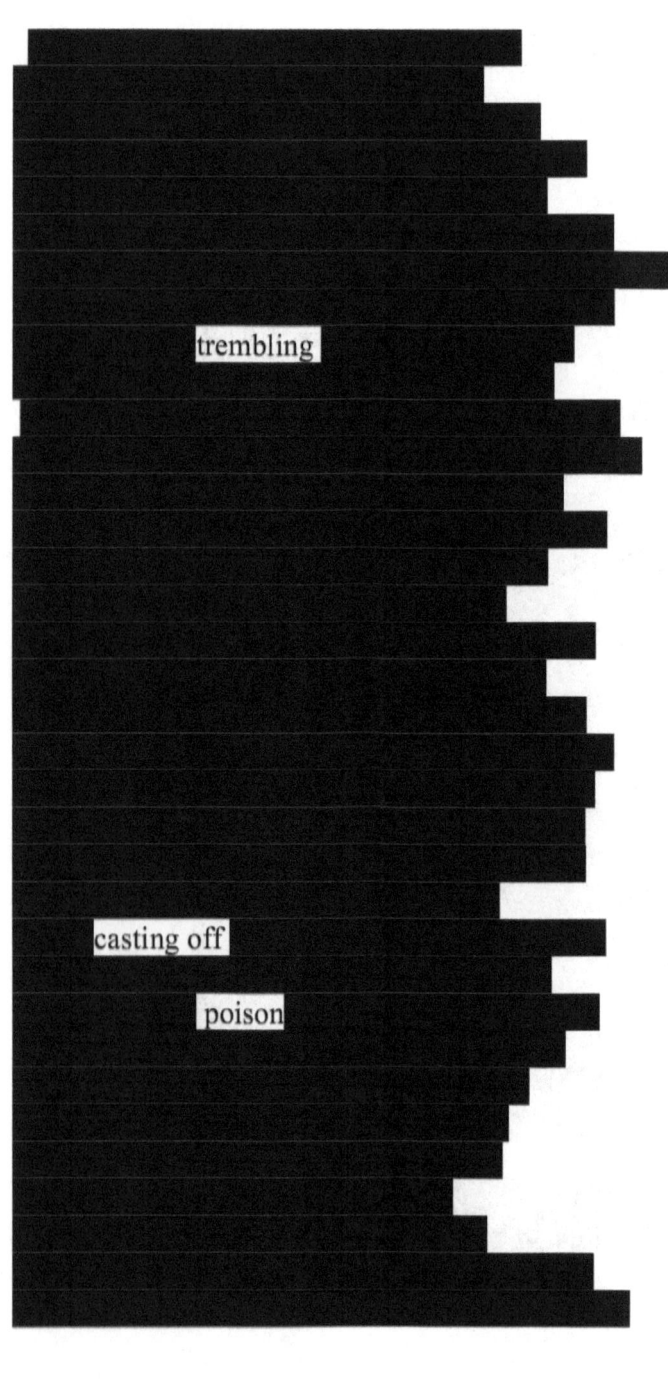

lonely secret

laments

shrieks

ruined

useless
weight

Despairing

gasping
death
shaking   anger

                an insolent delight;
a son's death

            the god he feared,
The laws of nature

Pitied
    me

a nameless thing.

forsaken
abandoned
alone,
Deserted
with despair

this madness,

this unmanly rage
you forsake
your helpless father yet survive

this destruction
while I dissolve

Enlightened

resolute to die

Rather than exile and old age

Loathed by   god   lingering

Myself, my wife,   my family,

Our prayers, our tears,   are vain.

And you conspire to be slain,
relentless
Reeking with blood-

I stand resigned,

With   rage

By   religion

                    your guilt
        impious holy   to bear,

        unequal

        dark

                        seized with fear,
Not for myself,
            ruined

hostile

deserted

Deceived

mad

Abandoning   forgotten

horror
the silence
With some small glimpse of hope

longing

exiled

Resolved,

I yield to Fate

happier

uncertain

spring

I leave

I lay the foundation

with horror

bloody
Mute

I atone,

I bent my knees
violated

faithless decline

mournful
dejected
tepid

friendly
needful weary

sad relics

sound
dark
Undaunted

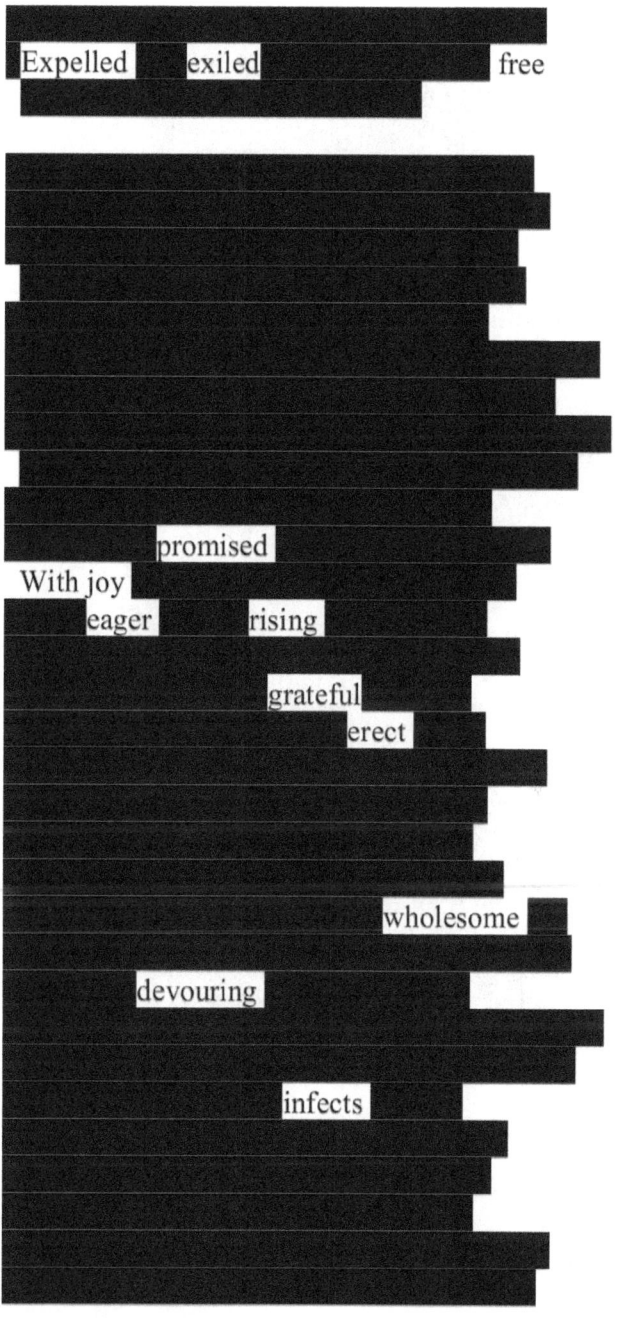

Expelled   exiled   free

                promised
With joy
    eager   rising
                grateful
                    erect

                        wholesome
        devouring

                infects

flaming
bright

troubled

companions

Astonished   voices

a clammy sweat

and shivering

revives   my mind

mad

head

scattered
face
            roaring
              in the dark.

ascending
rude   whirling

Monsters
From hell
With virgin faces,   obscene,
Foul

with hunger

defiling
loathsome

holy   altars

from the dark recesses

odious

monsters

mangled

native

promised
curses

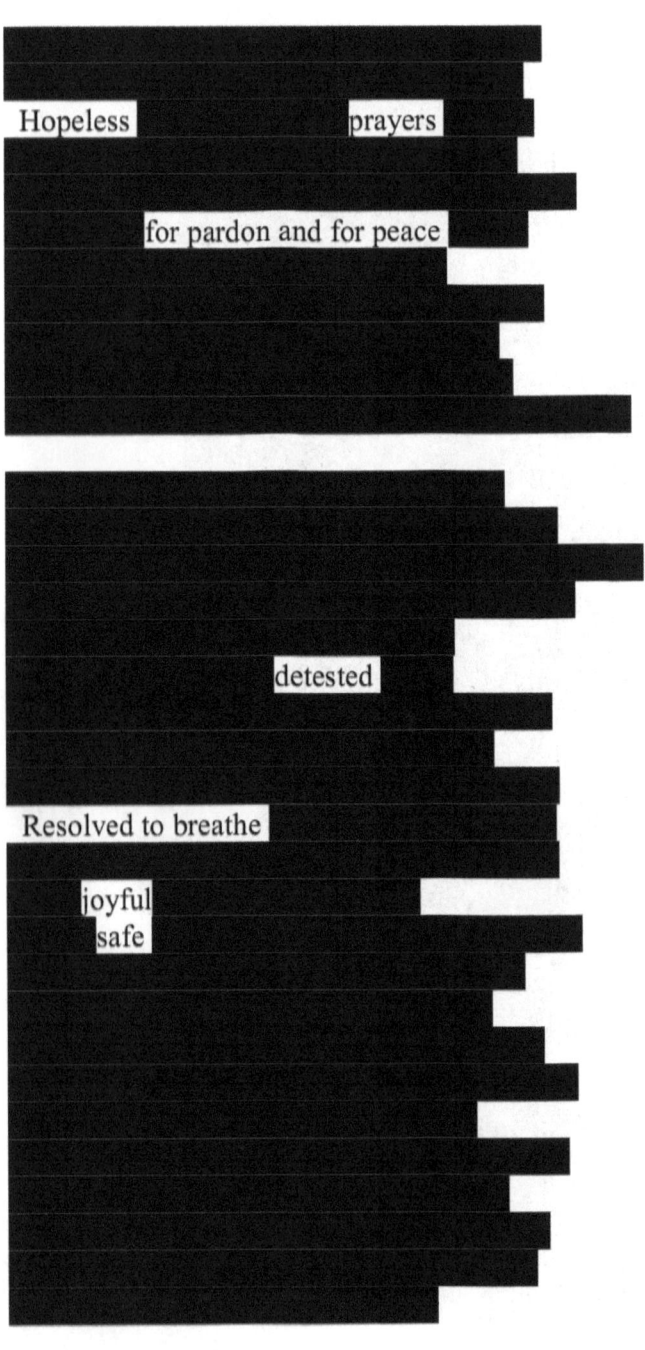

Hopeless prayers
for pardon and for peace

detested

Resolved to breathe
joyful
safe

happy

Are you alive

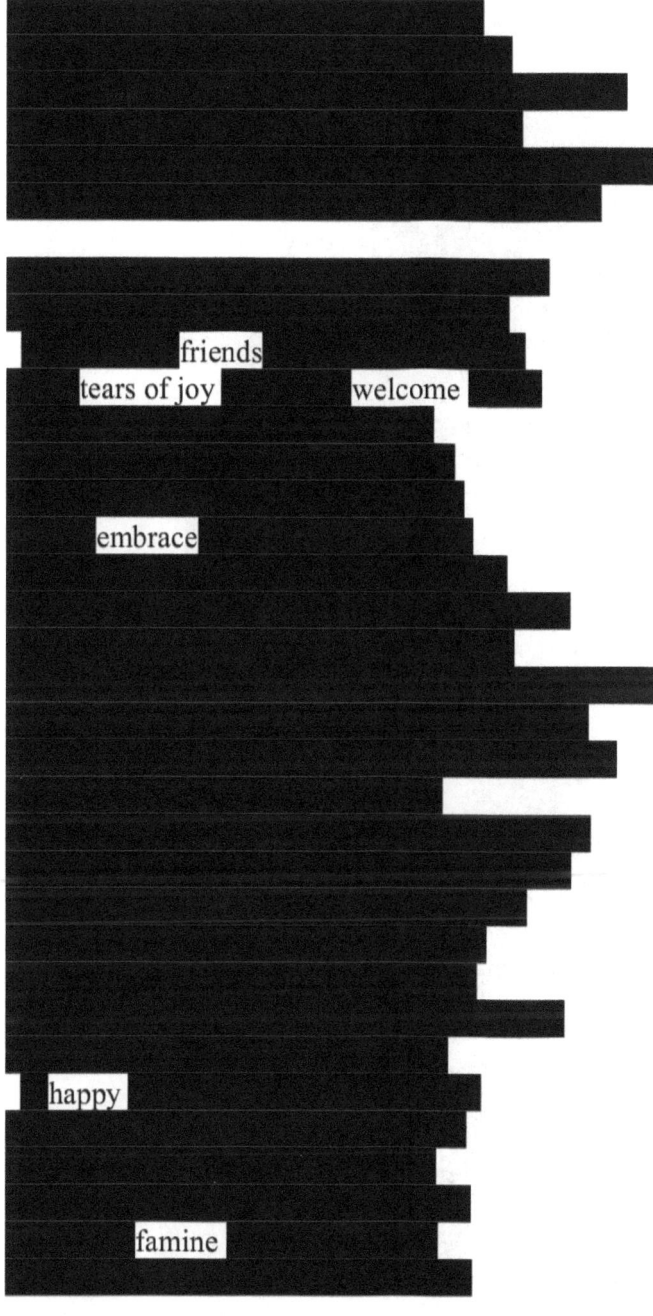

awful dread.

struggling

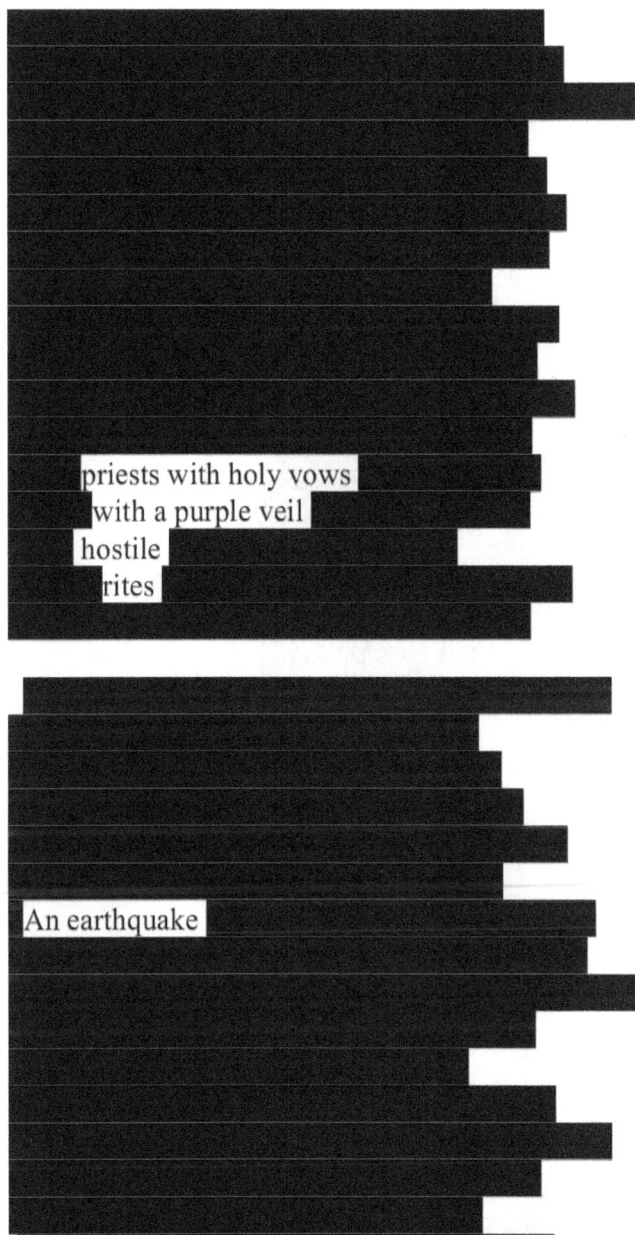

priests with holy vows
with a purple veil
hostile
rites

An earthquake

with fury

madness of the visionary
with loud curses

willing   to write

to find

peace

sweeping

auspicious

words embraced

with love
preserved life when lost,

forbidden

distance concealed

with useless words

With tears

Avoiding

Deluding visions

obnoxious

happy

birth

withdrawn
dusky

declining

threatening

rising

sound;

raging
swelling
gales

complain
in vain.

Peace may succeed

we hear   surly sound

down to hell

secure

liquid lakes of burning sulphur

bellowing sounds and groans

implore

frightful

tears

unhappy

death
for this abandoned life

I die content

encouraged.

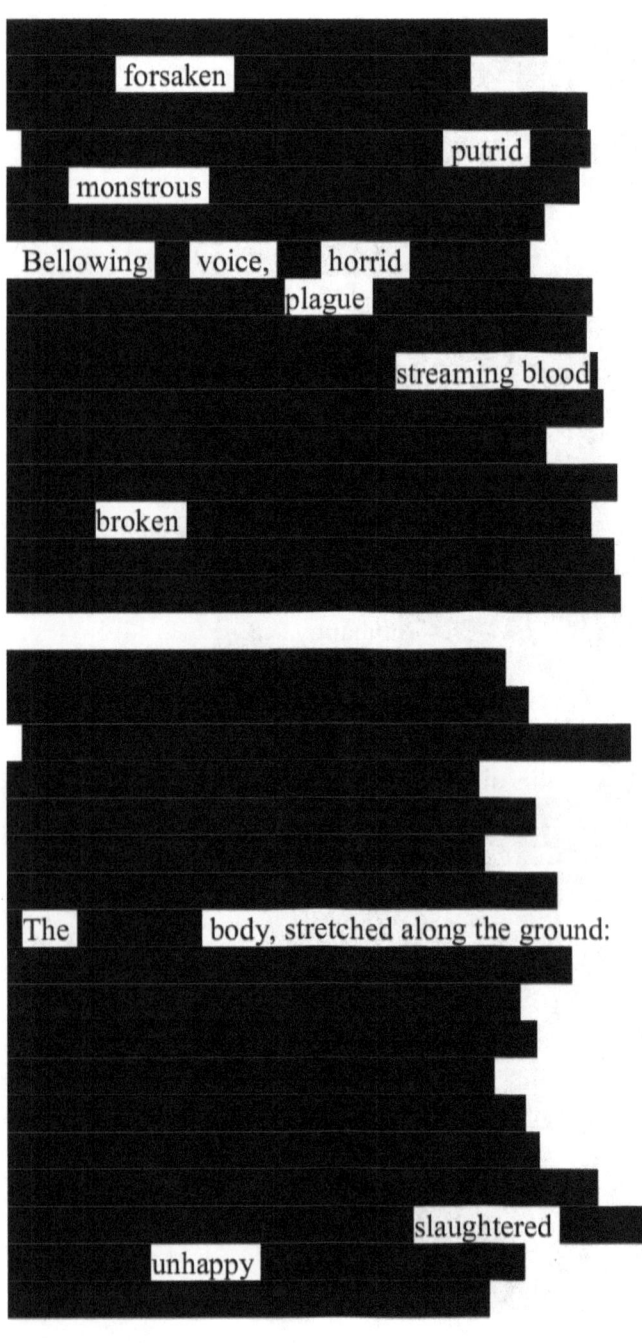

hated

I hear his thundering voice

longing

all I ask, this cruel
death

solace

with a sudden fear
and silent haste

the dreadful cry
the bellowing noise

the friendly gale

free from fear

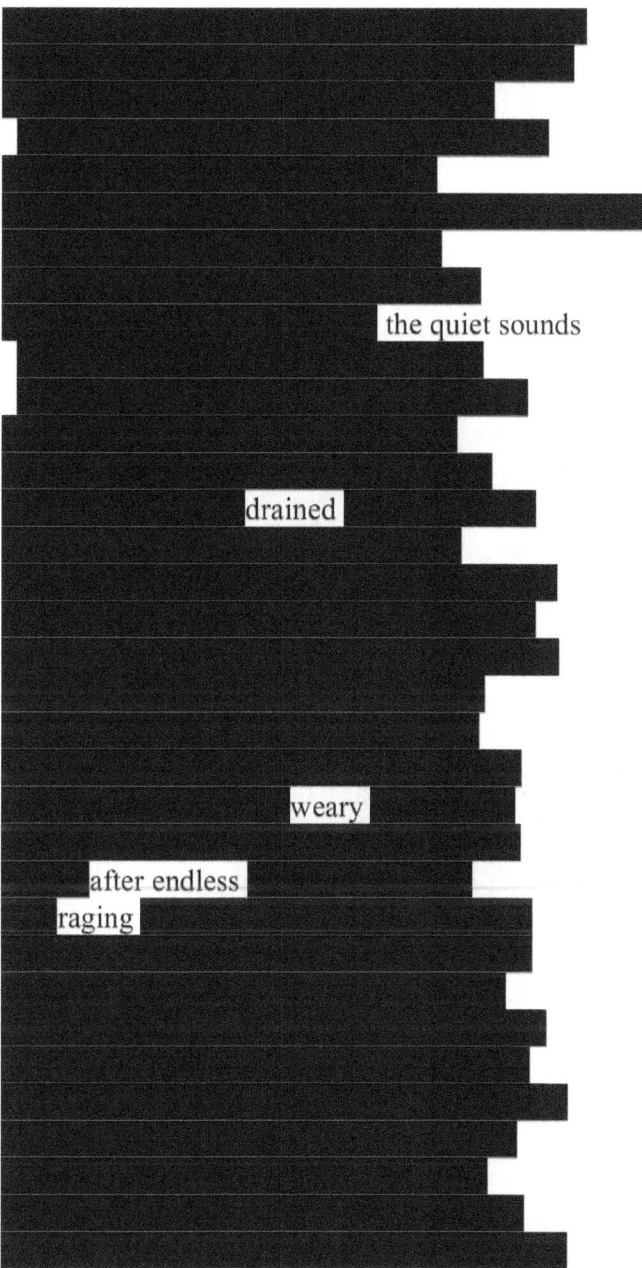

the quiet sounds

drained

weary

after endless
raging

anxious cares

inspire

passion

mournful

dreams

degenerate

attempts

to confess my frailty, to my shame,

Condemned

life,
Without joy
pompous
sorrows

Sick

Wounds   random
Distracted with   pain
                seeks the silent
                      fatal

        faltering

                the   band,

wishes

closely

slow

majestic

goring
Impatiently feeble

obscure
lightning

torrents

enlighten
Hell from below
howling conscious

death

raged against god revengeful

phantom

peaceful universe

Dissolved abandoned

unwelcome

celestial

holy
blood

disdained
Mad despair
on the sacred altars

thoughtless

scorning me,
banished

restore to light

beaten

god descends
precipitated
along the flood

Degenerate

foreign
Forgetful

severe

pleasure
rising

fate
god
vanished out of sight.

offended

To suffer

pleasure

forsake
impatient
impotent

excuse
ungrateful

compassion

despairing

raging

holy

faith

would lead me to

the promise

angry   dreams

defrauded

I leave you

guilty

outrageous threats

hardened

Faithless

exile
hungry

peaceful

black
death

shall spread

loathing

Resolved

growing

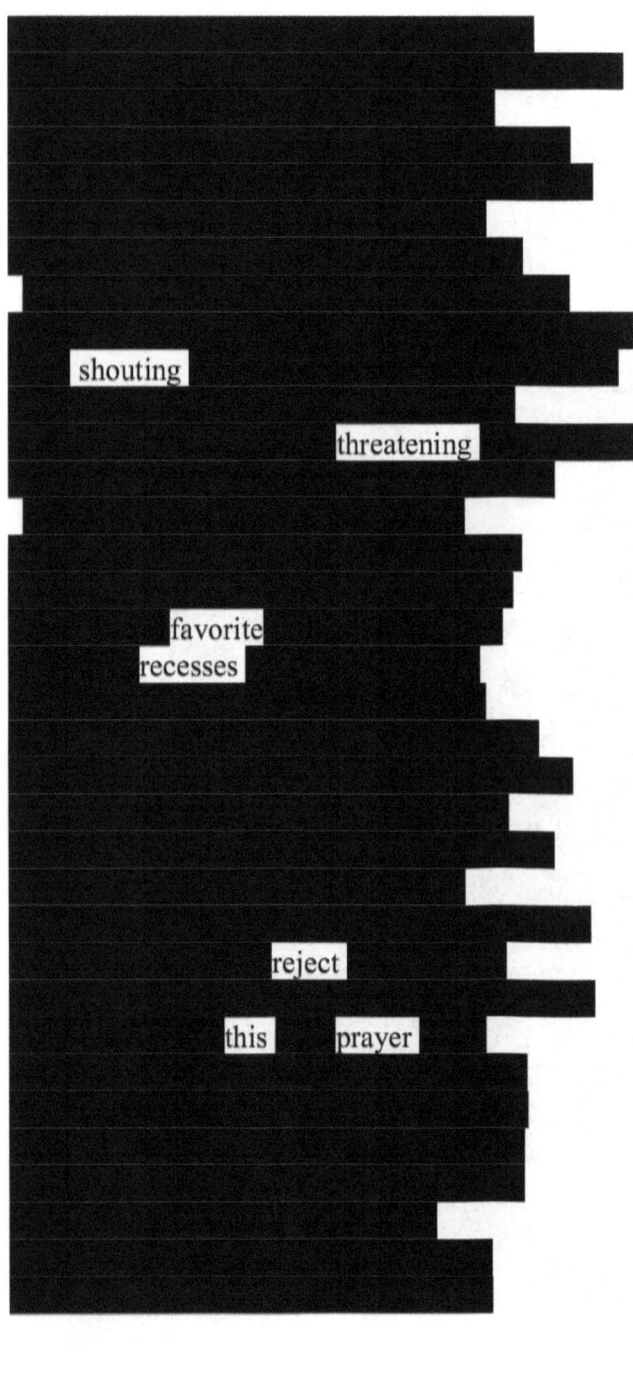

shouting

threatening

favorite recesses

reject

this prayer

inured to
pity
My death

is refused again.
god stopped love.

Unmoved,

the

cruel
hate,

putrid

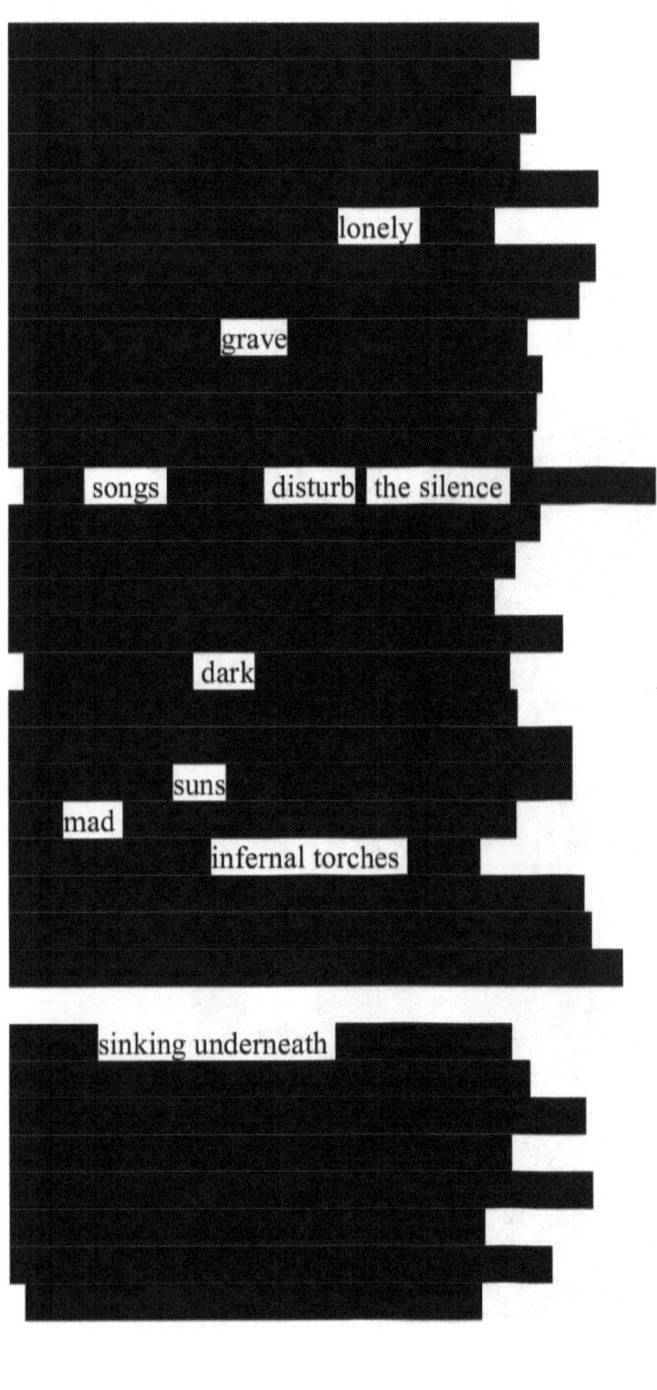

soothed   into sleep

relics

secret funeral

concealed

Sad

brazen

Robbing the mother's love
obscene

dying
conscious

silent

Avoiding love I found despair

disturbed

near a hostile town

a furious hate
dire
obstinate

blazing
rage

god commands

Destroyed
the reeking boy

extinguished   faithless

peaceful
discouraged   expelled

the cruel war

my dying
curse
Perpetual hate

on my grave

And the same hate descend on all our heirs!

atoning

disastrous
fire

furious

pain
approaching death

left behind

Repressed

anguish

reeking

spouting blood   streaming

sounding

groans

furious despair

destroyed me

sickened

struggling   life dissolved

his voyage

shining

empty

heaven

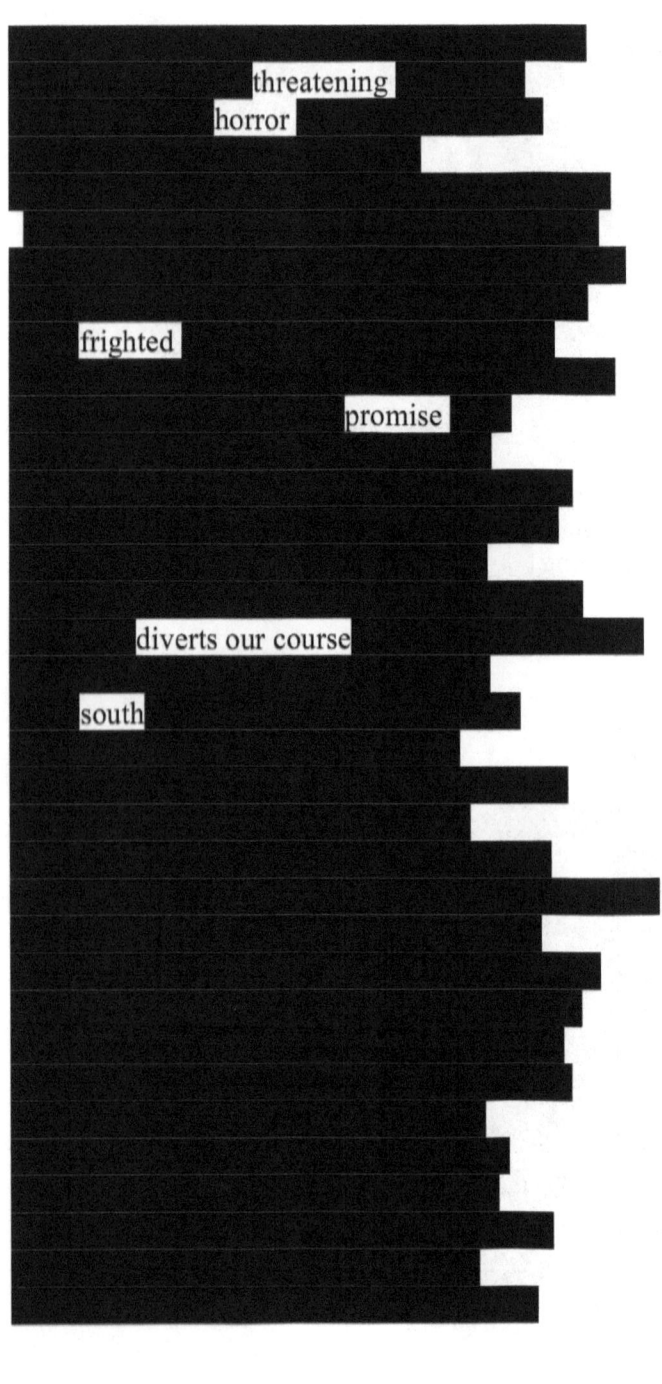

ethereal
rising
I celebrate

our voyage to renew

The sacred monster
With harmless play

generous

hell

Within the circle

Exact

fierce

Cries

Amidst the loud applause

advancing

In triumph

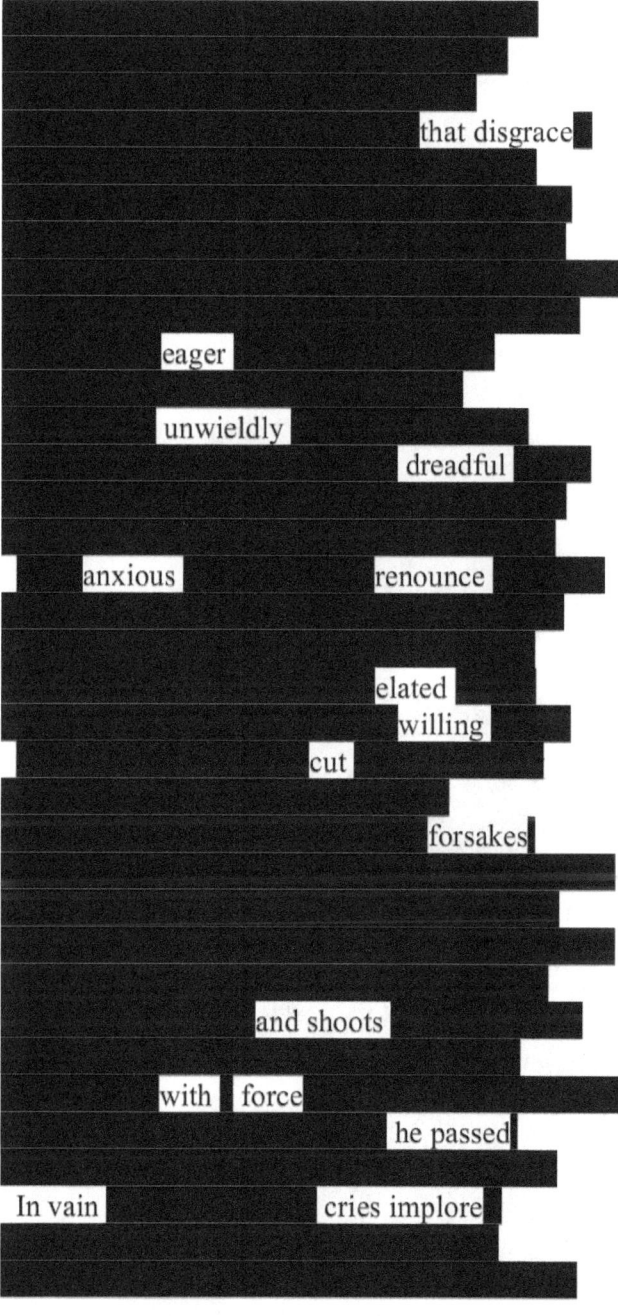

that disgrace

eager

unwieldy

dreadful

anxious   renounce

elated
willing
cut

forsakes

and shoots

with force

he passed

In vain   cries implore

Applauding   shouts

grudged

obstinate to die
  with success,

          guilty

    grateful

virgin

trembling

In vain

cries.

loaded
seized

conquering

delivered to fame

Shot

spent
eager

Soaked with blood newly slain.
careless
where the puddle lay
on the floor
He fell

falling is to rise

his face,
smeared with blood

in triumph

loud applause echo

funerals
by the stroke of his hand,
And drew the wonder of the gazing throng.

Not one dares answer

I resign

Stripped

bent

provoke

different

rattling

warping

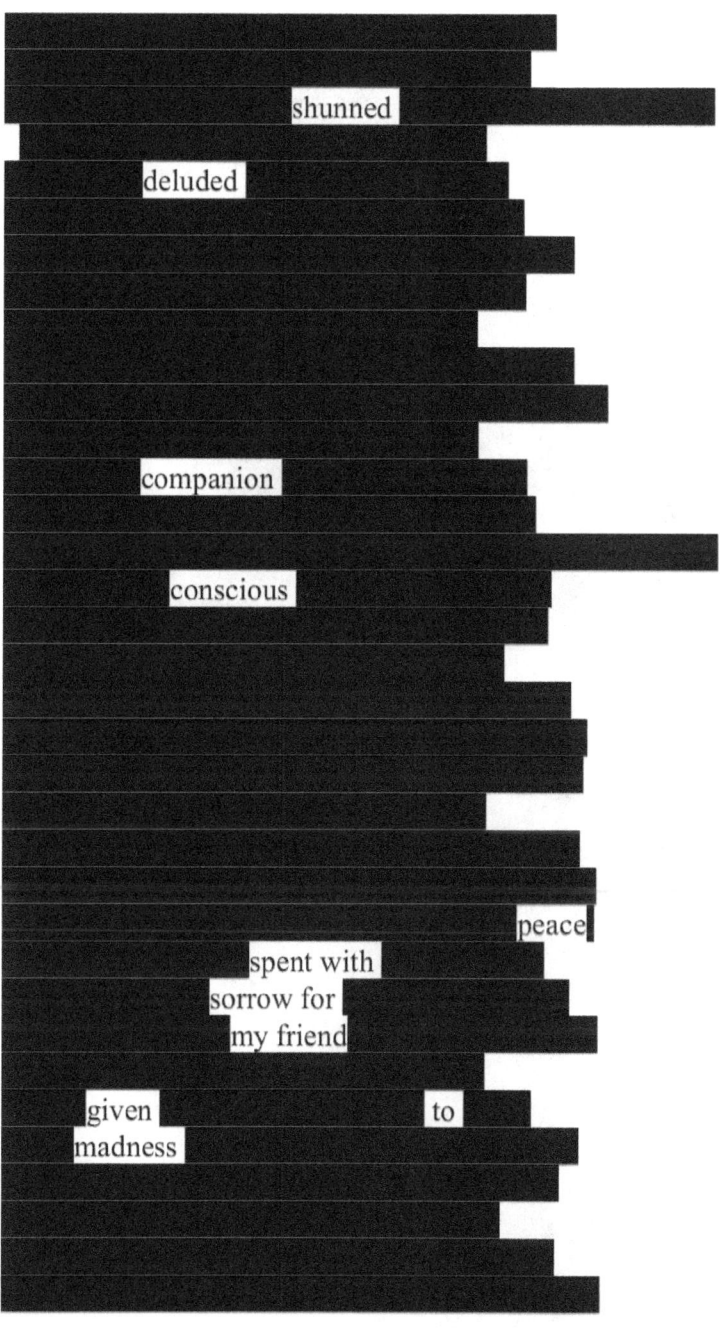

And hung his head

The deadly stroke   pierced the skull.

It flew whizzing
and the shouting cries
Of the people
made a shot, that cut the cord
released

The fatal message

childish
grace

calling out,
withdrawn, an open
youth

Shouts of applause resound from side to side.

Each brandishing

honors
White

age

in
hopes and fears   in their face

With harmless rage

　　　　　　in　friendly
　　　　ways
　　weary
　　　　　　denied
Turned
　　　in the deep

　　succeeding　　　graceful art

　　sacred
　　　　　　　ancient hate
　　　the dead

　　　　revenge

alone
With   tears

Implore god for peace

Wandering in exile
   search in vain

       endless

                doom

voice
What madness

your   hopes

smoldering
destruction
The silent plague

fall alone on me!
the willing sacrifice

doubtful
Forgetful
experienced
resigned

secrets
old　　useless

dangers

disturbed　mind.

vital breath,

my careful ghost

damned
　　Elysian

loud laments
Of parting friends
                    degenerate
        desire

                            the rage,
The   sufferings
Compel
        pity

As if it were

the causes of hatred
But you can witness its effects too well.
You saw the storm

And rebellion

with execrable flames

For what remains, your god I implore

your love

dashed against the walls
with bodies of the slain

fear no more,
　　　　　　　　　one　　　　　alone
Shall perish

God
Descends
　　　　his destined prey
　　he takes his fatal way.

the monster

drunk

insulting

daemon
faith
the navy
infamous

grieved
Deplored his death   his pain
                doomed   to lie.

greedy joy

hollow

Deep

heavy

cut

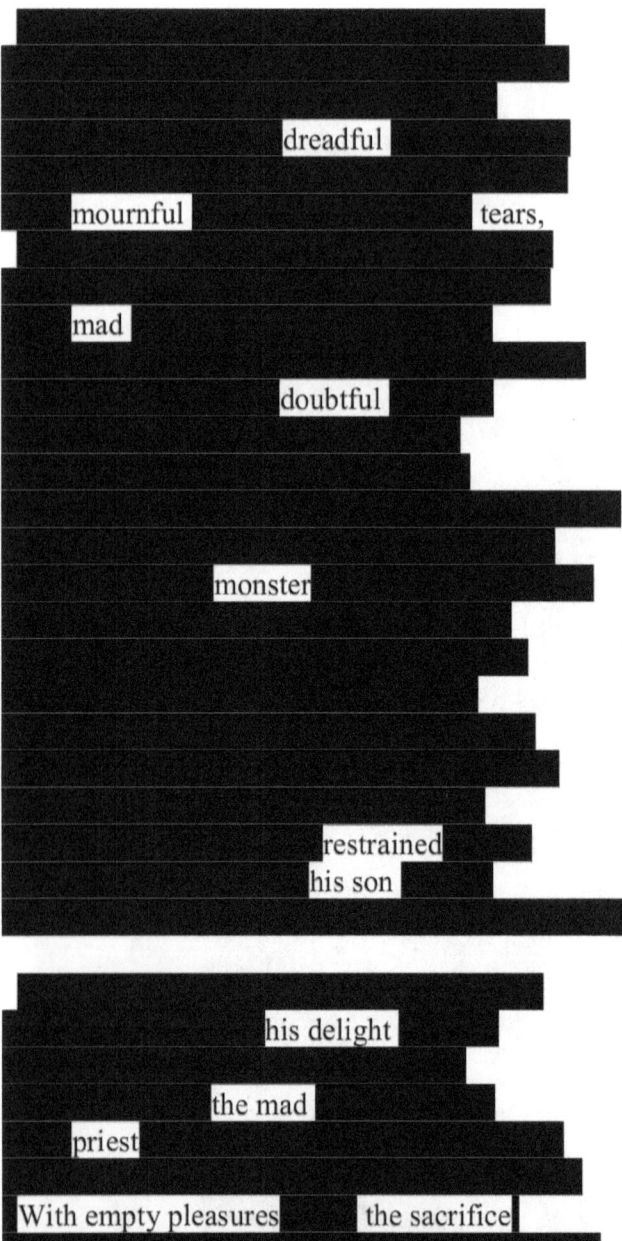

"Why this delay?"

dumb

holy fear

unwilling to destroy

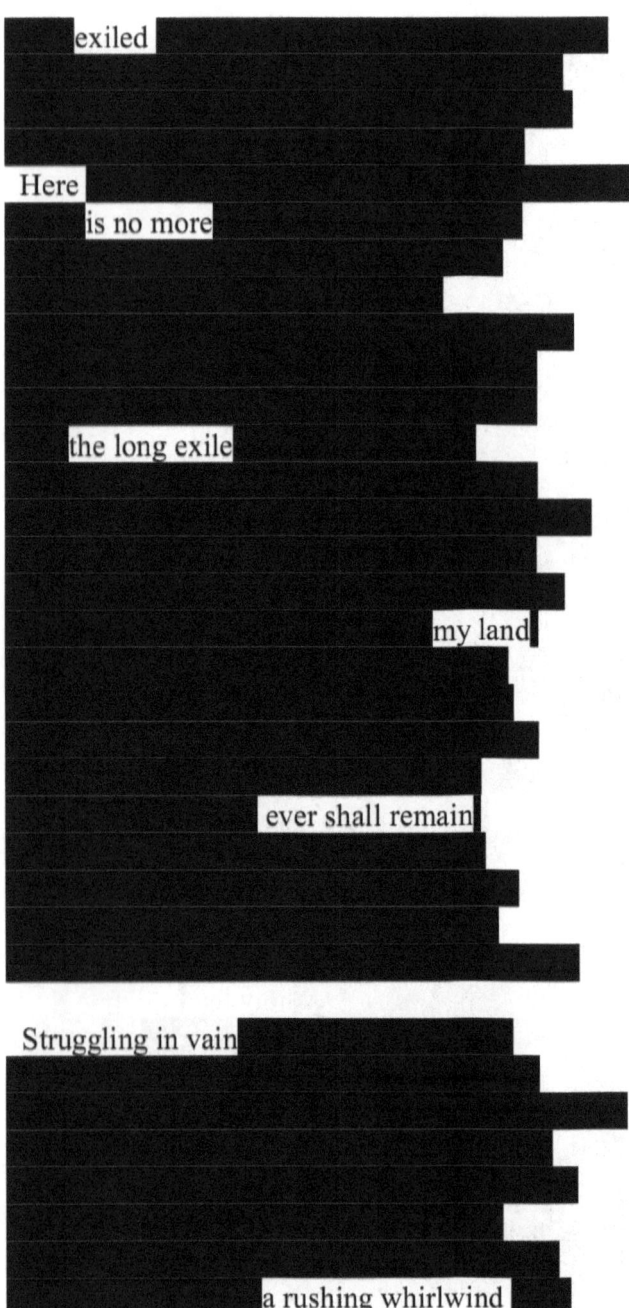

exiled

Here
is no more

the long exile

my land

ever shall remain

Struggling in vain

a rushing whirlwind

purple

hostile
strange

a foreign guest

ambiguous
    mysterious
  truths

                              the road
To hell lies open

enchanting

descent

The gates of hell are open night and day

impenetrable
infernal

Following

unworthy fate
he lies   unburied
Deprived
the dead

peace
of discontent

grieving
            fruitlessly

God

              was   near
              but

He now provokes

his mangled carcass

to perform the funeral

He knew the sacred ground

deathless fame

performed

a gloomy

stench
that infects

sacrifice

Invoking
hell

With holocausts

profane

along the gloomy space

mystic wonders of

the waste   of the dead.

malignant

skies

of hell

With anxious Pleasures of

this infernal

dream

horrid

The sacred

rejected

penance

repressed,

quiet

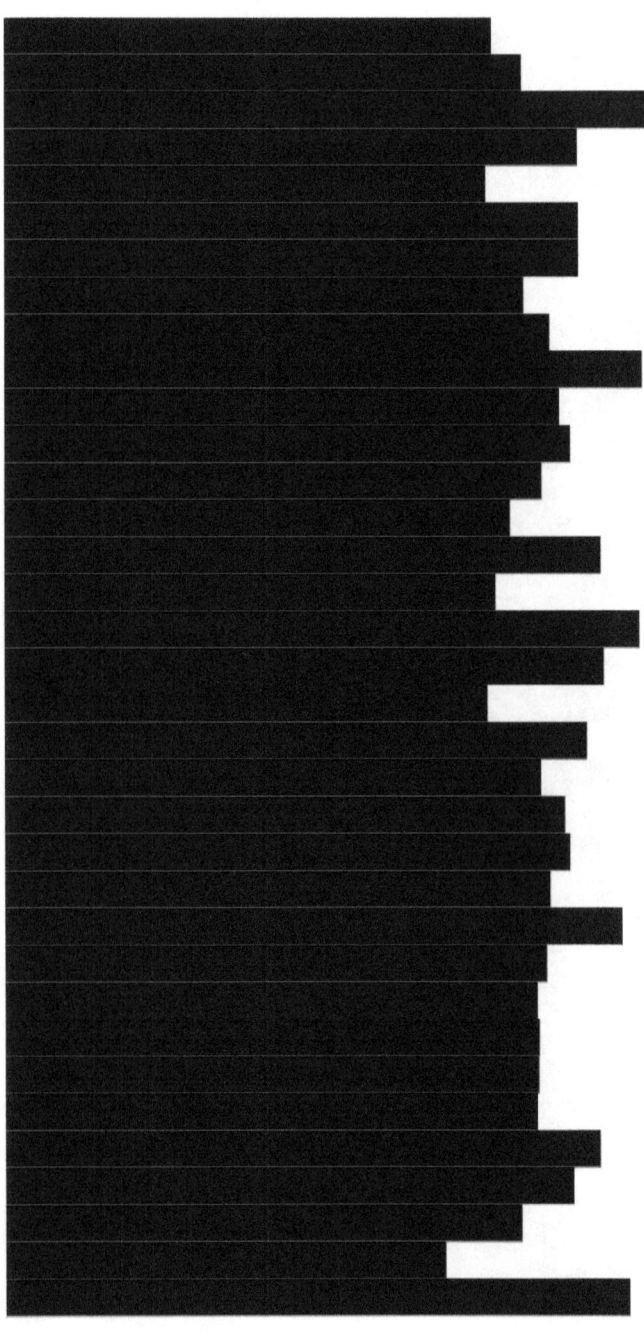

Saved

A privilege

so light
rising

Emboldened by despair

Resolved on death, he dissipates his fears,

bold

young

Brave

standing

Transfixed

inspiring

Proud
Vaunting defied

what madness
You find

No part of life is free

time changes all changes us

We live and delight

Sing and howl

With patience or revenge

gracious

demigods
This is the way to heaven
From this beginning

breathing

worthy son

Undaunted

hardened

free;

Astonished awake

inspired

confusion

frantic

securely

the fool who sought his destiny
Mad
For   death
These are not

hostile   hope

with calm
fate

equal

lucky
blind desire
to pursue

friends

found within

with courage   he sung
              his delight

                with rage and grief

To save the living, and revenge the dead

Forsaking honor, and renouncing fame

They cannot conquer, they oppress with weight.

he presses on

the invader

Battered and beaten

succeeds

heaven summons all

inferior

peace

Solicits hell

hospitable
fugitives

Be free
live
let me save the son

a rejected boy

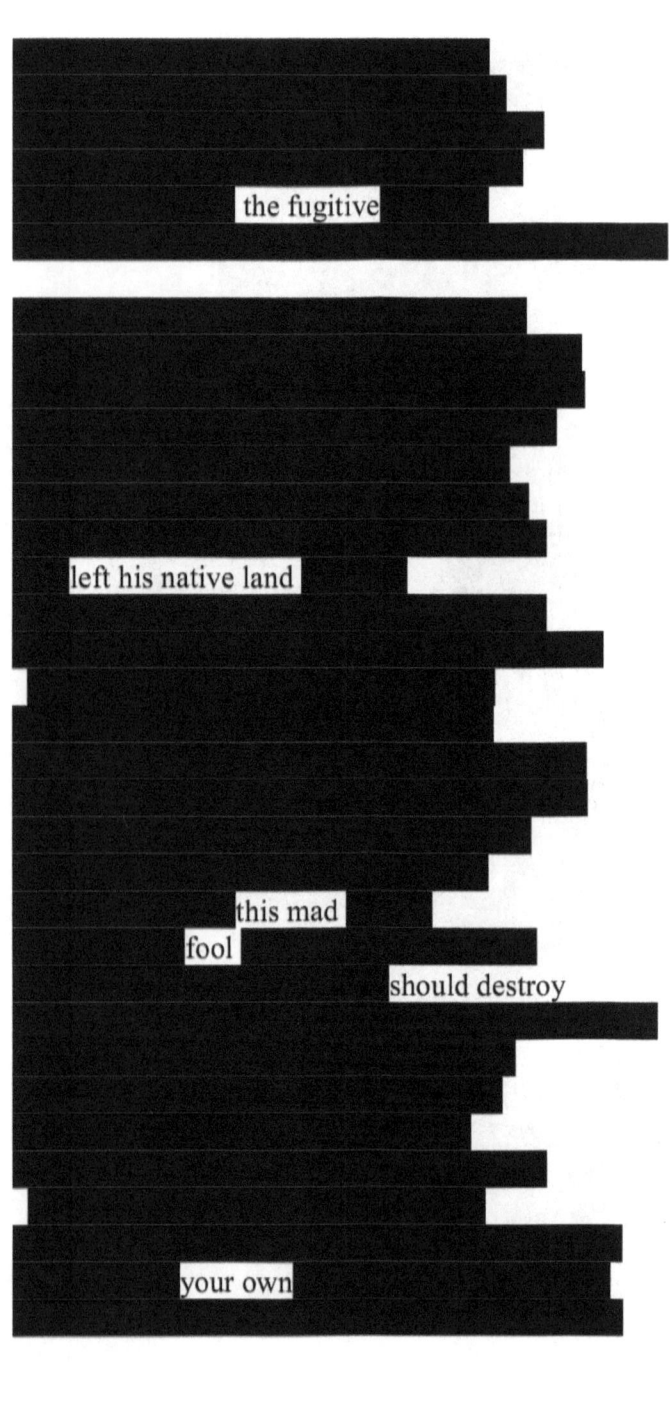

peace

exiled
Was I the cause of mischief?

too late

immortal hate

happy fate

hopeless of relief

deserved

care

death born

coming to

his own small strength

bold and violent

wandering

open

sing

exhausted

peals

unanimous

lineage

sung　　　　alone
to soothe his grief

chant　　in air

With lifted hands

Frowning
at the blast

murmuring

who closed his eyes

They know him from afar;

whose voice

fled   profane

And gave us life

By your insulting

Parting

Unknowing

lead us on

renewing

with loud shouts

sinister

undaunted

wish

Yours is the day

mindful

your fathers'
staggering

exposed

hated   hostile

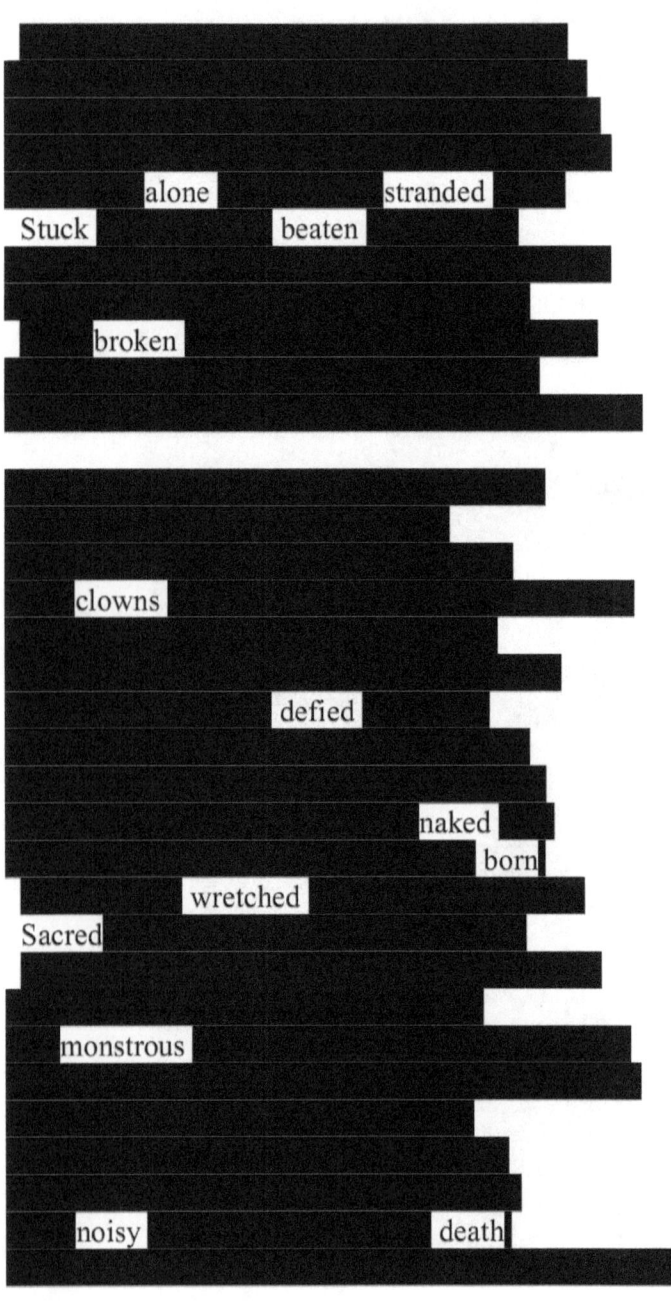

alone stranded
Stuck beaten
broken

clowns
defied
naked
born
wretched
Sacred
monstrous
noisy death

obscene

weapons

reached his heart

free
life

succeeds
Conspicuous

contending
With equal force

shameful
with grief

blood, and   brains together fly

destiny

                    a memorable death.

        hopes

        pressed
    angry weapons
Of   youth and beauty
            forbid to breathe   native air.

empty
Success
Alive or dead, I deserve a name
meditate
downward
Imagine

holy

blood

Around the walls

Now

shining

heart

bloody ground.

my message

costs him dear
lifeless body

the shining

mournful night

insulting

fate

grace   restored

But sad

whirls

living sacrifice — relentless remorse

shone amidst
proud

magic
impenetrable
spheres,

Exulting
defense
drags him down
the prostrate wretch

unpitied

monsters

fled

silent

Defied the lightning

With strength

With fury

pushing
mad
headlong

torrents
raged

long

immortal

anger

reprieve

you sought so long

shelter

the delusion
a life redeemed
With honor

for what offense

What will they say

their dying groans

draw me down alive

Sometimes

pity
repressed his rage

on him, and him alone,

empty

face
receives his wound
he falls

Unthinking

savage

inspired,
just revenge

Proud as a hungry lion

dying faintly

death

overcome
gods from heaven
And mourn the miseries of human life.

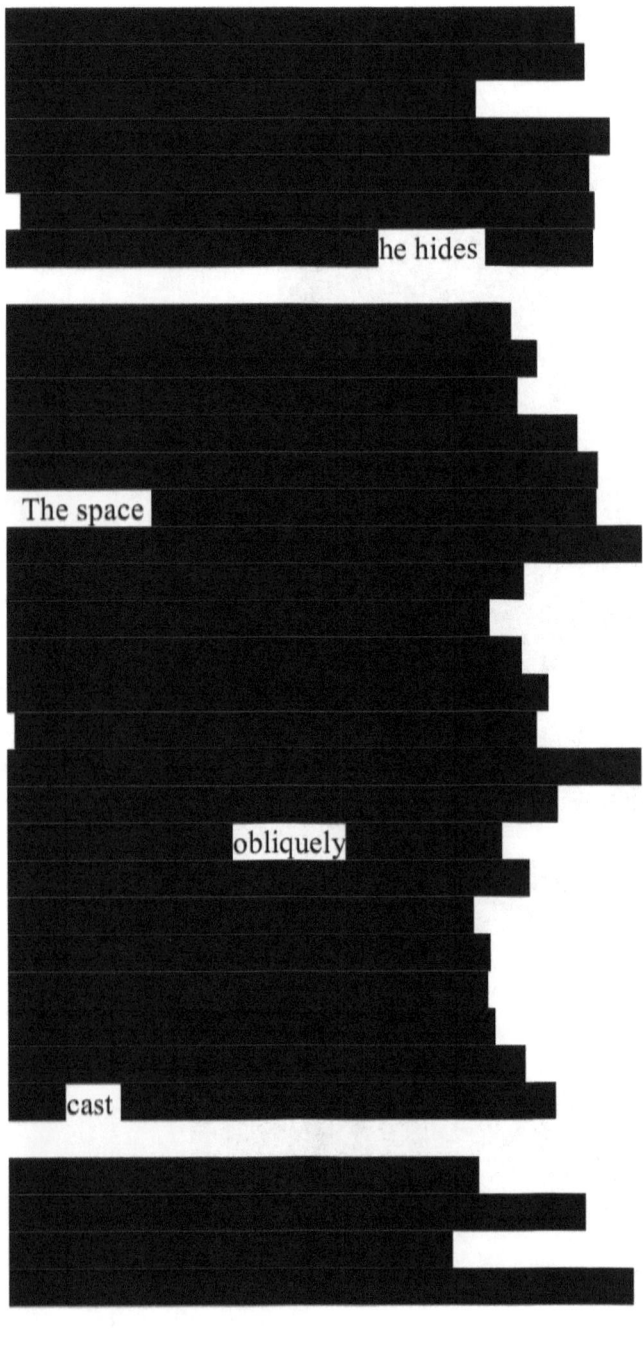

he hides

The space

obliquely

cast

with grief

sing

useless
to save himself

Shouts of applause

a storm
held at bay

ground

with anguish

drooping
grisly

danger

far off

resign
His life

                                        abandoned, and exiled

                                                from their hate
And yet I live
Of hated men, and of more hated light:

Love, anguish, wrath, and grief, to madness
Despair

raged

god

spoke no more

my business is to die

Scarce

cares
his friend
first   performed

rising

in triumph
hung on high,   from afar,
sacred to   God

smeared with blood

my friends
performed

no more   fierce   lies
a sacrifice

your happy
ignorance

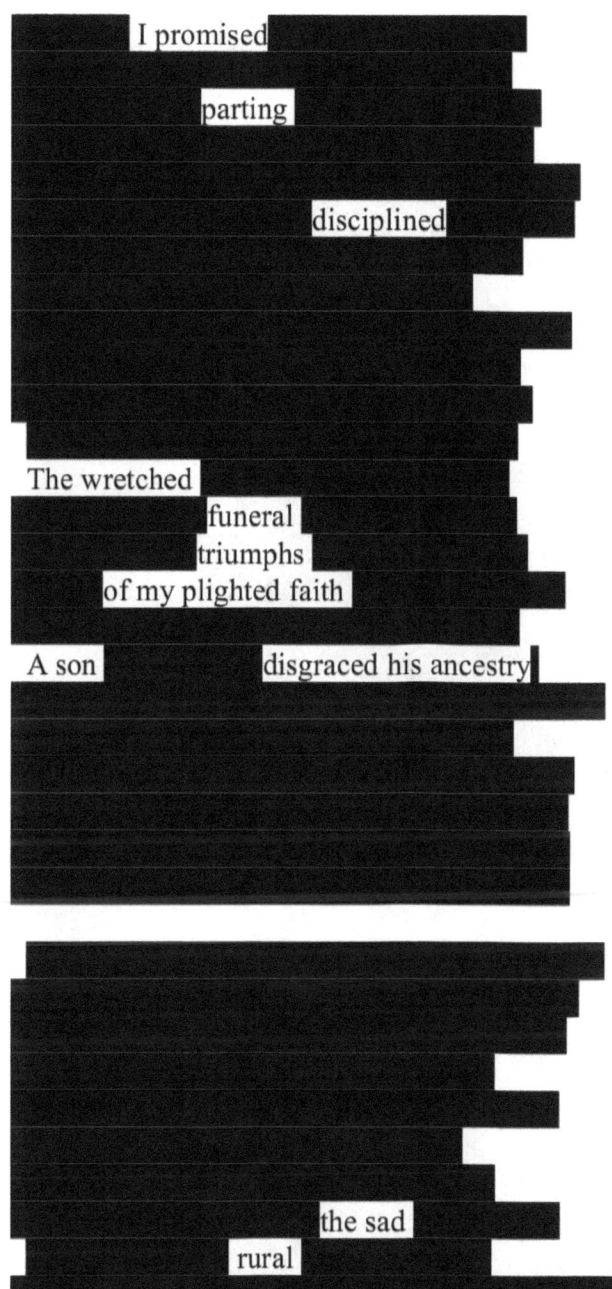

I promised

parting

disciplined

The wretched
funeral
triumphs
of my plighted faith

A son   disgraced his ancestry

the sad
rural

earth

wrapped around his head
the yellow hair
catching fire

in sorrow
he sinks upon the ground

the hoarse sound

gave a vent to grief

All hate was ended in death

a man
Who sought friendship

Fell without fault

This is the way to restore the peace

Long hate
Broke silence first

your friend

proud

no longer foes prepare
To forget

the fatal news

disordered

Young

Prelude

leaving me behind

Beyond   nature

my   friend

It was not his fault
But my own crime, for having lived too long.

I expect
all that he can give
Joy is no more; but I would gladly go,

drums   mournful sound.

wasting

heaven

unhonored

promiscuous

shadows

Perform

sorrow

with spite

deaf to

peace

anxious

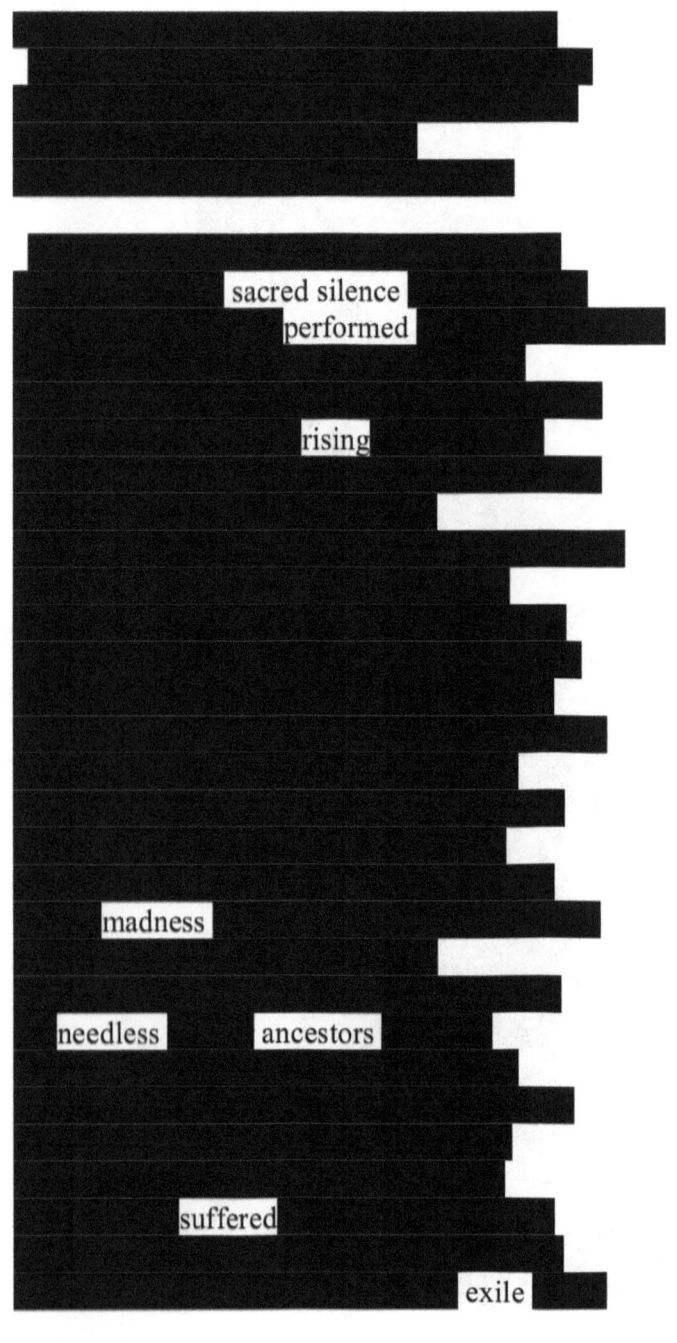

sacred silence
performed

rising

madness

needless   ancestors

suffered

exile

Outcasts, abandoned by   Heaven
despised

expelled

My much loved country
I mourn

squalid

remains

hopes must center on ourselves alone

there,

let'em build and settle, if they please

for a lasting peace

peace

I know

to withdraw

exhausted

with awful dread

in confusion

peace   calls
fierce
scornful

disordered

distracted

encouraged

By nature

To drive   downward

Would trust open

strength

I wish
salvage
had been my celestial train,
since
death

By whatever hand

unpunished from

my

native land

Black clouds and stormy winds

Approach

Advancing in a line

                                    the shouting
    distance

                          with a mighty shock

                                    lightning
He rolls   in blood, and breathes his last

Driven

          backward
Repulsed

                                    repelled.

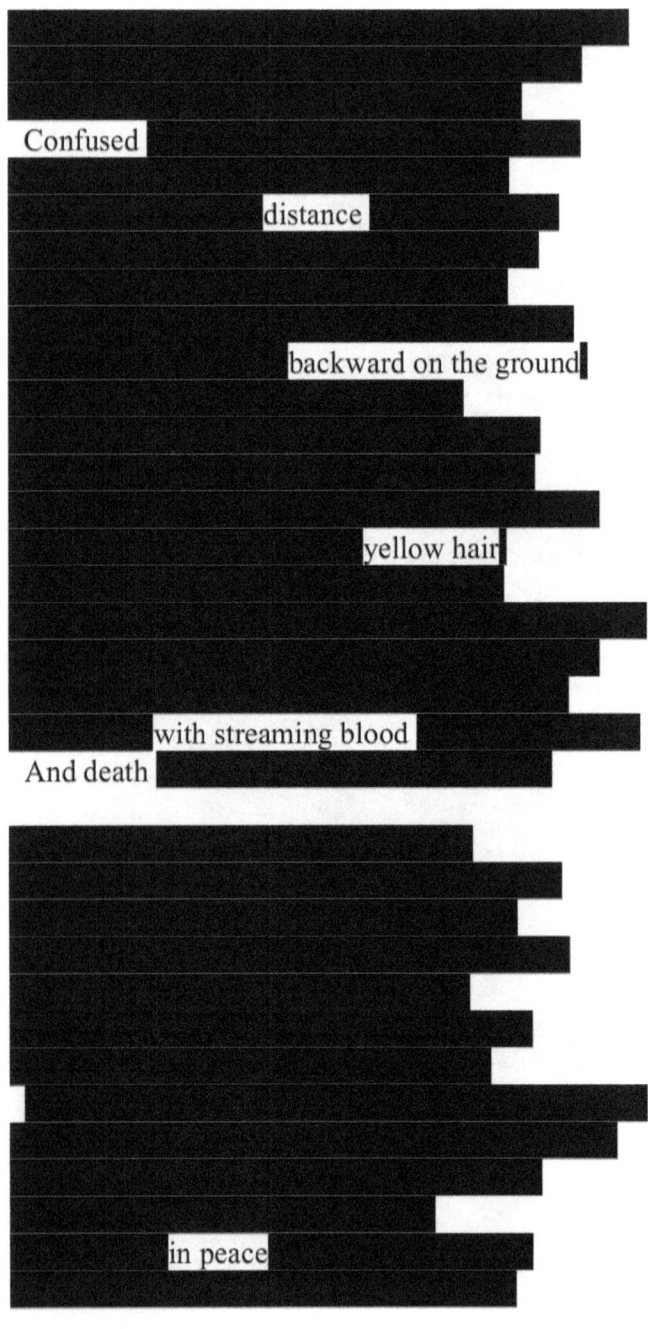

Confused

distance

backward on the ground

yellow hair

with streaming blood
And death

in peace

The weapon falls,
He groans,
Brains, mingled with his blood, smear his face.

What courage have you shown

fool
Caught in the train

With   lies

with disdain
abandoned

ambitious

The stains of this dishonorable day

the death desired

Directed by the sound

deeply drunk

trembling
fear confused with

Conscious

agonizing

my last words

Despair and rage

The

Sacred place with oaks

To mark

An honor

of death,
His friend

lost

escape

the sight of home

friends excluded

Blind

valiant with despair

for   freedom

now freed

From secret

distance of the space between.

questioned hate

makes a sour retreat

No more excuses or delays: I stand prepared to desert native land.

Now let me speak with patience from a heart free my kindness would not be denied,

I promised my

honor

I feel you have had your share.

put an end to
unresolved fate
death a lasting peace

god is not near
an empty cloud

living

twisted

peace

With sighs and tears

God
took his
hope

if I fall
renounce
all questions of
peace.

hell signs the peace

I swear:
I touch the flames

An orphan now,
dishonored

desponding

With eyes dejected, and with trembling hands;

A livid deadness

But you,

rising

With tedious   new souls

fail   to foment   rage
With lying

foreign   I lead the way
               impious

               forced to

Run madly

With equal
Peace   and hate

                eager

with a scornful smile
god   found a fitter sacrifice.

stupid
heavy endless

naked
truce:

altered minds
violate the peace!

Resolved

unwilling

from my example learn

happier chance than mine

the hostile sound

pouring on a plain.

Afterword

My first book, *Epitaph,* was a flarf diary of the five weeks after the death of my father in January of this year. The impetus for this second book was the death of my grandmother just five weeks later. In this way, though the two books differ in form and process, this book can be seen as a continuation of *Epitaph.* (The first draft of *Epitaph* was completed on the day of my grandmother's funeral).

My relationship with my grandparents was difficult. A petty, stupid conflict erupted twenty years ago that effectively ended our relationship, sadly, as we never spoke again during their lifetimes. We were products of different times and different worlds, and the two worldviews were apparently irreconcilable, particularly with regard to religion. The conflict ultimately led to a collapse of the extended family, and I found myself as a young man leaving Chicago to start over in North Carolina.

My grandmother's wake and funeral were disorienting experiences, seeing family and hearing stories that at the same time were familiar and utterly foreign to me. I felt as if much of my life history was hidden or blacked out.

Describing this feeling to my brother, I made the offhand comparison to the *Aeneid.* Back at work, following my usual routine of blacking out extraneous details from my schedule using a Sharpie, I hit upon the idea of telling the story of the conflict with my grandparents, the subsequent dissolution of the family, and my starting a new life and family in North Carolina as a blackout poem using the *Aeneid* as a source text.

As work progressed on the book, the 20th anniversary of the death of Kurt Cobain approached, and I found myself hearing his music in a new way. I recognized in Cobain's music pain and anger that dovetailed well with the old feelings brought up by attending my grandmother's funeral, and it became clear that Cobain belonged in the DNA of the work. The title, *Come As You Are,* is of course the title of one of Nirvana's hits, but it also stands in contrast to the central theme of the conflict whose story this work endeavors to tell. "Come as you are" is also a slogan found on banners of many churches here in North Carolina, encouraging people to come even if they choose not to wear their Sunday best- highlighting the religious conflict at the heart of the story. I found that Virgil provided surprising references to Cobain's songs, particularly "Come As You Are," "Lithium," "Pennyroyal Tea," and "On A Plain," unexpectedly cementing Cobain into the work. Lastly, referencing Kurt Cobain and Nirvana sets the book clearly in the early 1990's, the setting of both the height of Cobain's fame and the dissolution of my extended family.

This is a highly personal work, but it is not pure autobiography. The protagonist, like in *Epitaph,* is an unstable "I." In the work I recognize myself as a lost young man, ostracized and exiled twenty years ago. I recognize an image of Kurt Cobain gleaned from his songs, interviews, and stories told about him in the media. Quite to my surprise, I also recognize an old friend (to whom this book is dedicated), who like Cobain was another musician who died at age 27 and who suffered dearly in the last years of his life after the death of his father.

It was not until after the first version of *Come As You Are* was released as an e-book that I became aware of Tom Phillips and his masterwork *A Humument*. His book might be the most engaging, entertaining, fun, fascinating book I have ever read. It is a work of pure genius, and I am convinced, though I did not know of his work beforehand, his work influenced mine, through others who practice blackout poetry. Imagine how startled I was to read his first page! ("I sing a book of the art that was of mind art though I have to hide to reveal. Now read on.") I clearly owe Tom Phillips a debt of gratitude. I also owe a debt of gratitude to Kenneth Goldsmith for pointing me to Tom Phillips and *A Humument.*

I would like to thank you, the reader, for taking the time to read this work. I hope you found it as enjoyable to read as I found it to create.

> \- Mark Snyder
> June 8, 2014

In Loving Memory Of

Arline E. Alberts

Born December 12, 1924
At Rest February 24, 2014
Mass of Christian Burial
Monday, March 3, 2014 - 10:00 A.M.
St. Bernadette Church
Interment St. Mary Cemetery
Evergreen Park, Illinois
Lot: 33   Block: 2   Section: KN   Grave: 2

I am home in heaven, dear ones; Oh, so happy and so bright! There is perfect joy and beauty in this everlasting light. All the pain and grief is over, every restless tossing passed; I am now at peace forever, safely home in heaven at last. There is work still waiting for you, so you must not idly stand; Do it now, while life remaineth- you shall rest in God's own land. When that work is all completed, He will gently call you Home; Oh, the rapture of that meeting, Oh, the joy to see you come!

HICKEY MEMORIAL CHAPEL
442 E. Lincoln Highway • New Lenox, Illinois

Acknowledgements

I would like to thank Dr. Greg Newby, Chief Executive and Director of Project Gutenberg for his support and for permission to use their work as a source text. Project Gutenberg is an incredible resource and well worth supporting.

I would like to thank Therese Pope for her collaborative partnership and friendship.

I would also like to thank Nicola Quinn, Karen Carlson, Mary Armour, Mark Herron, and T. de los Reyes for their encouragement and friendship, and for reviewing several sections of the draft as it was in progress.

I would like to thank Julia Bloch for her assistance and advice early on in this project. Thank you also to Steve McLaughlin for his assistance with formatting issues.

Thanks also to Kenneth Goldsmith, for his support and encouragement and for his teaching on uncreative writing which is written into the DNA of this book.

I am as always especially grateful for the friendship, mentorship, and encouragement of Al Filreis. I've said this before, but this book simply wouldn't have come to be without you.

Thank you to my brother David Snyder, for his encouragement, and for being family.

Thank you to my daughters Hayley and Melanie, who inspire me to be the best father I can be, and who lovingly forgive my shortcomings.

Finally, I am very grateful to my wife Pamela, who understood my need to do this work. Your love and encouragement was essential. I don't know how I got so lucky, and I love you very much. And thanks for putting up with me having "Lithium" on repeat for hours.

Mark Snyder grew up in Evergreen Park, Illinois. He serves as a Community TA in the course in Modern and Contemporary American Poetry at Coursera.org under Prof. Al Filreis. His first book, *Epitaph*, was written in early 2014. He has also created two albums of experimental music- *Necessary Evil* and *Requiem*- the latter a secular conceptual setting of the Mass composed in the days immediately prior to the death of his father. He lives in rural North Carolina and practices general community psychiatry. He lives with his wife and daughters.

www.ingramcontent.com/pod-product-compliance
Lightning Source LLC
Chambersburg PA
CBHW020052200426
43197CB00049B/134